World's Greatest
MUSICIANS

Wonder
House

(An imprint of Prakash Books)

(An imprint of Prakash Books)

contact@wonderhousebooks.com

ISBN : 9789388810388

CONTENTS

A.R. RAHMAN

BIRTH: January 6, 1966
Chennai, Tamil Nadu, India

A.R. Rahman is an Indian singer, songwriter and music producer. He is also called the "Mozart of Madras" by his fans. He is known for synthesizing Indian classical music with electronic.

Allah Rakha Rahman was born as A.S. Dileep Kumar on 6th January, 1966 in Chennai, India. His father, R.K. Sekhar, was a Tamil musician who composed for the Malayalam film industry. He started to learn the piano at the age of four. He used to assist his father in the studio. Rahman was nine years old when his father passed away. He was brought up by his mother, Kareema Begum. His mother used to rent out musical instruments to earn a living. Rahman played many instruments, but he was particularly fascinated with the synthesizer.

At the age of eleven, Rahman started playing for the orchestra of Malayalam composer, M.K. Arjunan. He trained under Master Dhanraj. He obtained a scholarship to study at the Trinity College of Music, London due to his experience. He obtained a degree in Western classical music from Trinity College, Oxford.

Rahman started his career by creating jingles for advertisements. He has written more than three hundred jingles. His jingle for the advertisement of Titan watches became quite popular. Director Mani Ratnam approached him to compose the soundtrack for his Tamil film, Roja, in 1992. This was Rahman's first hit soundtrack. He was awarded the Rajat Kamal (Silver Lotus) by the National Film Awards for

Roja. Rahman also started Panchathan Record Inn studio in his backyard. It would later become the most advanced recording studio in India. Other hit soundtracks by Rahman include *Bombay, Kadhalan, Indira, Minsara Kanavu, Swades, Rang De Basanti* and *Guru*. His debut in Bollywood was in Ram Gopal Varma's *Rangeela*, in 2005.

Andrew Lloyd Webber, a British composer, hired Rahman to compose music for his Bollywood-themed musical, *Bombay Dreams*, in 2002. In 2003, he composed the score and soundtrack for the Chinese film *Warriors of Heaven and Earth*. In 2006, Rahman composed the score for the musical version of *The Lord of the Rings*. He also composed the soundtrack for Spike Lee's *Inside Man*. The music score for Shekhar Kapoor's *Elizabeth: The Golden Age* was co-written by him and Craig Armstrong. Rahman also composed the music score in Danny Boyle's *Slumdog Millionaire*, in 2008. He received the British Academy of Film and Television Arts (BAFTA) Award, a Golden Globe, and an Academy Award for this composition. In 2010, he also won a Grammy Award in the category 'Best Soundtrack' and 'Best

Song'. The song, "Jai Ho" reached number fifteen in the US Billboard Hot 100. Rahman has also composed scores for films such as *127 Hours, Rockstar, Raanjhanaa, Highway* and *Beyond the Clouds*. In 2017, Rahman debuted as a director and writer for the movie, *Le Musk*.

Rahman has received many awards and honors. He was awarded the Padma Bhushan, the third-highest civilian award, by the Indian government in 2010. He has received four National Film and six Tamil Nadu State Film Awards. Rahman has also been honored with the Jayalalitha Award by the Government of Tamil Nadu. He has been awarded fifteen Filmfare Awards (North) and fifteen Filmfare Awards (South). In 2006, Stanford University awarded him for his global contribution to music. Rahman received an honorary doctorate from Berklee College of Music in 2014.

He was part of the *Time's* list of the '100 Most Influential' people in 2009. He is also referred to as "Isai Puyal" ("the musical storm" in English) by his South Indian fans. In 2013, a street was named in his honor at Markham, Ontario, Canada. The government of Seychelles made Rahman the Cultural Ambassador of Seychelles in 2015.

Rahman was appointed as the ambassador of the Stop TB Partnership in 2004. He supports Save the Children India. He also composed "Indian Ocean" along with Yusuf Islam in 2005. The sales of the songs were donated to people affected in the 2004 tsunami. Rahman started KM Musiq Ltd. in 2008 to train young musicians. The theme music of the 2008 film *The Banyan* was composed by him, to aid poor women in Chennai. Rahman, along with Sivamani, composed the song "Jiya Se Jiya" in support of the Free Hugs Campaign in 2008.

Rahman married Saira Banu in 1995. They have three children.

ARETHA FRANKLIN

BIRTH: *March 25, 1942*
Memphis, Tennessee, USA

DEATH: *August 16, 2018 (aged 76)*
Detroit, Michigan, USA

Aretha Louise Franklin was an American singer, songwriter and actress. She is called the "Queen of Soul". She ruled the age of soul music in the 1960s.

Aretha Franklin was born in Memphis, Tennessee on March 25, 1942. Her father, Clarence LaVaughan Franklin, was a Reverend of a Baptist church. Her mother, Barbara Siggers Franklin, was a gospel singer. Franklin had three siblings and grew up in a religious family. At the age of six, Aretha's parents separated, and when she turned ten, her mother passed away. Aretha taught herself to play the piano and sang for her father's church choir. She began her career in music at the age of fourteen. Her first album, 'Songs of Faith', came out in 1956 with J.V.B. Label. Franklin signed a recording deal with Columbia Records and moved to New York in 1960. Her song "Today I Sing the Blues" topped the Hot R&B Sellers charts.

She also released her pop album, 'Aretha: With The Ray Bryant Combo' in 1961. It became an instant hit with its single "Rock-a-bye". Her hit singles from 1964 to 1966 were, "Runnin' Out of Fools", "One Step Ahead", "Cry Like a Baby" and "You Made Me Love You". Franklin began recording with Atlantic Records in 1966. She released 'I Never Loved a Man the Way I Love You' in 1967. It topped the Billboard Hot 100. Her albums 'Aretha Arrives', 'Lady Soul' and 'Aretha Now' earned her the title of "Queen of Soul". Her singles, "Respect", "Think" and "I Say a Little Prayer", gained her international recognition. Franklin received two Grammy Awards for "Respect".

During the 1970s, the singer released 'Spirit in the Dark', 'Young, Gifted & Black' and other such albums. Franklin recorded her first live album titled 'Aretha Live at Fillmore West' in 1971. Her 1972 album, 'Amazing Grace', became the best-selling gospel album of the time. She also gave the soundtrack for the film *Sparkle* in 1976. In the 70s, Franklin won six consecutive Grammy Awards, the last of which was for her single "Ain't Nothing Like the Real Thing" in 1974.

Franklin signed with Arista Records in 1980. She performed for the Queen of England in the same year at the Royal Albert Hall. Also, her single "United Together" ranked third in the R&B charts. She made an appearance in the musical *The Blues Brothers*. In 1981, her album 'Love All the Hurt Away' was released. Her duet song with George Benson called "Hold On, I'm Coming" earned her her eleventh Grammy Award. She worked with

Narada Michael Walden for her 1985 album 'Who's Zoomin' Who'. It became her first platinum album. Its single "Freeway of Love" earned her another Grammy. Franklin released another gospel album in 1987, titled 'One Lord, One Faith, One Baptism'. Her 1998 album, 'A Rose is Still a Rose' was certified gold. Franklin's autobiography *Aretha: From These Roots* was published in 1999.

Franklin released her album 'Aretha: A Woman Falling Out of Love' from her label in 2011. In 2014, Franklin released a cover of Adele's "Rolling in the Deep". After this, she became the first woman to have one hundred songs in R&B charts.

Franklin has received eighteen Grammy Awards in her lifetime. She has won three American Music Awards in the category 'Favorite Soul/R&B Female Artist'. She was the first female musician to be inducted to the Rock and Roll Hall of Fame in 1987. She became the most charted female artist of all time. She also received the Presidential Medal of Freedom in 2005. The same year, she became the second woman to be inducted to the UK Music

Hall of Fame and the Michigan Rock and Roll Legends Hall of Fame. She has also been inducted to the GMA Gospel Music Hall of Fame. She was ranked number one in *Rolling Stone* magazine's list of '100 Greatest Singers of All Time' in 2010. She was honored as the MusiCares 'Person of the Year' in 2008.

Aretha Franklin has been married twice. Her last marriage was to Glynn Turman in 1978. They separated after six years of marriage. She was a mother to four children. Her third son, Ted White, Jr. (Teddy Richards), also became a musician.

Franklin passed away on August 16, 2018, due to pancreatic cancer. She was 76 years old at the time. She continued recording and performing until the very end. In 2009, Franklin performed "My Country 'Tis Thee" at the inauguration of President Barack Obama. She has been described as "the voice of the civil rights movement, the voice of black America." In 2014, Asteroid 249516 was named "Aretha" in her honor.

BILLY JOEL

BIRTH: May 9, 1949
The Bronx, New York, USA

Billy Joel is an American singer, songwriter and pianist. His most famous single is "Piano Man". He released several hit songs in the 1970s and 1980s.

Billy Joel was born as William Martin Joel on May 9, 1949, in Bronx, New York. He was raised in a German-Jewish family. His father, Howard Joel, was an acclaimed pianist. Joel also had a sister and a half-brother. Billy Joel started learning the piano under the guidance of Morton Estrin and musician Timothy Ford. Joel left high school to pursue his career in music. The first band he joined band was called The Echoes. Joel recorded some of his instrumental pieces with them. In 1967, Joel left the band to join The Hassles. This band had signed with United Artist Records. They released two albums but didn't gain any commercial success. He left the band in 1969 and formed a duo with Joe Small called Atilla. They recorded an album with Epic Records in 1970. However, this duo did not last long either.

Joel signed a solo contract with Artie Ripp's Family Productions in 1971. His debut solo album, 'Cold Spring Harbor', released the same year. The album didn't perform well, and its quality was questionable.

In 1972, Joel started playing the piano at a piano bar. He played under the pseudonym 'Bill Martin'. Joel composed his legendary single, "Piano Man" during this time. Late in 1972, Joel's recording of "Captain Jack" was played on a radio station in Philadelphia. It became a huge chartbuster in the East Coast. As a result, Columbia Records offered Joel a record deal. He recorded his album, 'Piano Man', with Columbia Records in 1973. It became his first gold album. Joel's 1977 album, 'The Stranger', was one of his most commercially successful albums. It was also Columbia's biggest selling album. It had four singles in the US Billboard Top 25. His next album was '52nd Street'.

Joel performed at the 'Havana Jam Festival' at the Karl Marx Theatre in 1979. His 1980 album, 'Glass House', topped the Billboard Album Chart for six weeks. He released his live album, 'Songs in the Attic', in 1981. It contained songs from his first album and some other early compositions. In 1983, his album 'An Innocent Man' was released. His first album, 'Cold Spring Harbor', was re-released by Columbia Records in the same year. His hit singles from the 1986 album, 'The Bridge', were "Matter of Trust" and "A Modern Woman". 'Greatest Hits' came out in 1985. It became the third most-selling album according to the Recording Industry Association of America (RIAA).

Joel received a Grammy Award for his 1989 single "We Didn't Start the Fire". He released his last pop album named 'River of Dreams' in 1993. His popular singles from 1997 were "To Make You Feel My Love" and "Hey Girl". His 2001 album 'Fantasies and Delusions' contained his classical compositions on the piano, the only one of its kind. In 2006, Columbia Records released '12 Gardens Live' that had songs from Joel's concerts at Madison Square Garden. Joel performed a free concert in Rome for his European tour. He performed the National Anthem at Super Bowl XLI in 2007. His album 'All My Life' was released the same year. It was his first pop album since 1993.

He received two Grammy Awards for his song "Just The Way You Are" in 1978. For his album 'Live from Long Island', he won the Award for Cable Excellence (ACE) in 1984. He was awarded the Grammy Legend Award in 1991. In the following year, Joel got inducted to the Songwriters Hall of Fame. He was inducted to the Rock and Roll Hall of Fame in 1999. He was awarded the ASCAP Founders Award in

1997. His album 'Greatest Hits' was certified Platinum by the RIAA. He was honored with the James Smithson Bicentennial Medal in 2000. In the following year, he was awarded the Johnny Mercer Award at the Songwriters Hall of Fame.

Joel has held many benefit concerts. He established Charity Begins At Home in 1979, to fund charities working against child abuse, domestic violence, cancer and other such issues. In 2002, Joel was honored as MusiCares Person of the Year for his charity work.

Billy Joel has been married four times. He's currently married to Alexis Roderick since 2015. Joel is a father of three children.

BOB DYLAN

BIRTH: May 24, 1941
Duluth, Minnesota, USA

ob Dylan is an American singer and songwriter. He is believed to have revolutionized
folk and pop music.

Bob Dylan was originally named Robert
Allen Zimmerman. He was born to Abram and
Beatrice Zimmerman in Duluth, Minnesota, on
24th May, 1941. He was brought up in a Jewish
community. He got his first guitar in 1955,
at the age of fourteen. Bob Dylan attended
the University of Minnesota in Minneapolis,
in 1959. He would perform folk and country
music at local cafés in Minneapolis. He
named himself "Bob Dylan" during this time,

inspired by the main character from a popular Western television series *Gunsmoke*. He quit college in 1960 and went on to pursue music.

In the January of 1961, Dylan shifted to New York. His idol, Woody Guthrie, a legendary folk singer, was hospitalized there. He would visit him in the hospital regularly. Bob Dylan wrote 'Song to Woody' during this time. In 1961, Robert Shelton reviewed one of Bob Dylan's live shows in the *The New York Times*. Columbia Records signed him after the review. In the March of 1962, Bob Dylan's self-titled first album was released but it did not do well. His second album 'The Freewheelin' Bob Dylan' was released in the May of 1963 and was a big hit. The songs "Blowin' in the wind" and "A Hard Rain's A-Gonna Fall" were part of this album.

His third album 'The Times They Are A-Changin' became an instant hit and marked Dylan as the songwriter for the '60s protest movement. He was romantically involved with Joan Baez, who was an important figure in the movement, during this time. Dylan also wrote songs for her. Her famous song "Love is Just a Four-Letter Word" was written by Bob Dylan. The folk trio, Peter, Paul and Mary, came up with their version of Dylan's "Blowin' in the Wind" in 1963. It acquired the second position in Billboard Pop Singles Chart.

In the 1960s, Dylan was also involved with the Civil Rights Movement. His songs were politically charged and addressed social issues. His single "Like a Rolling Stone" was released in 1965. It instantly became number two on the UK charts. The release of his folk-rock and electric album 'Bringing It All Back Home' in January 1965 created a major backlash amongst his folk music fans. His album 'Highway 61 Revisited' was also released in 1965. He began his tour with the band (initially, the Hawks) in 1966. The same year, he got into a motorcycle accident in Woodstock in July and returned home to recuperate. For the next two years, Dylan disappeared from the industry. His next album, 'Nashville Skyline' combined country music with rock. *Tarantula*, a book written by Dylan was published in 1971. Dylan started his career in Acting in 1973, with *Pat Garrett and Billy the Kid*, directed by Sam Peckinpah. Dylan was also the music director for this movie. His hit song, "Knockin' on Heaven's Door", was created for the movie.

In 1974, another book called *Writings and Drawings* containing his lyrics and poetry was published. Dylan's 1974 album, 'Planet Waves', topped the charts and became his first number one album. The albums he released in the 1980s included 'Infidels', 'Biograph', 'Knocked Out Loaded' and 'Oh Mercy'. In 2004, his book *Chronicles: Volume One* was published by Simon & Schuster. It was supposedly meant to be a three-book memoir on Bob Dylan. In a 2005 documentary called *No Direction Home: Bob Dylan* directed by Martin Scorsese, Dylan gave his first full interview in twenty years.

Dylan received his first Grammy for the single "Gotta Serve Somebody" from the album 'Slow Train Coming' in 1980.

In 1982, he became part of the Songwriters Hall of Fame. In 1988, he was honored in the Rock and Roll Hall of Fame. He became the first rock star to receive Kennedy Center Honors, in the year 1997. His 1997 album, 'Time Out of Mind' won him three Grammy Awards.

In 2000, he won an Academy Award for "Things Have Changed". In the May of 2012, he was honored with the Presidential Medal of Freedom. He was awarded the 2016 Nobel Prize in Literature. It was the first time a musician had been honored with this prize.

Bob Dylan and Sara Lownds got married in 1965. They had four children together and got divorced in 1977. He got married again, in 1986, to singer Carolyn Dennis. They had a daughter the same year, after which they got divorced in 1992.

BOB MARLEY

BIRTH: February 6, 1945
Saint Ann Parish, British Jamaica

DEATH: May 11, 1981 (aged 36)
Miami, Florida, USA

Bob Marley was a Jamaican singer and songwriter. He contributed to popularizing reggae music in the world. He sold more than twenty million records in his lifetime.

Bob Marley was born as Robert Nesta Marley to Norval Sinclair and Cedella Malcolm on 6th February, 1945. His father died of heart failure when Marley was merely ten years old. His mother, Cedella, was a singer-songwriter.

Neville "Bunny" O'Riley Livingston was his childhood friend in Saint Ann. Livingston's father, Thadeus, and Marley's mother had a daughter, and thus the two families started living together. In the 1950s, Marley lived in Trench Town, considered to be one of the poorest neighborhoods in the city. Marley and Livingston dedicated themselves to music, and Marley's singing abilities improved under the guidance of Joe Higgs.

Marley produced a few singles in 1962 with local record producer, Leslie Kong. They included songs like "Judge Not", "Do You Still Love Me?", "Terror" and "One Cup of Coffee". Marley, Bunny Wailer (Neville Livingston) and Peter Tosh (Winston Hubert McIntosh) formed a group together in 1963, eventually named The Wailers. Beverley Kelso, Junior Braithwaite and Cherry Smith later joined the band. The record company owned by Coxsone Dodd produced their single "Simmer Down" in January,

1964. It topped the Jamaican music charts. Their irst album 'The Wailing Wailers', from 1965, contained the hit single "Rude Boy". In 1966, Junior Braithwaite and Beverley Kelso left the band. The band released its first international album, 'Soul Rebels' in 1970. It was in collaboration with recording artist Lee "Scratch" Perry. It contained songs such as "Trench Town Rock", "Soul Rebel" and "Four Hundred Years". In 1971, two of their popular albums were released, namely, 'Soul Revolution' and 'The Best of the Wailers'.

The Wailers released their 1973 album 'Catch a Fire' with Island Records. It sold 14,000 records. Their next album, 'Burnin', was released in the same year. It contained the hit single "I Shot the Sheriff". Eric Clapton released a cover of this song in 1974 and it topped the US charts.

Peter Tosh and Bunny Livingston left the band in 1974. Bob Marley started making music under the name of Bob Marley and The Wailers. The 1974 album, 'Natty Dread', included songs like "Rebel

Music" and "Revolution". The song "No Woman, No Cry" from the album 'Live!' was listed in the Top 40 in Britain, a first for the band. In 1976, the album 'Rastaman Vibration' was released.

Its single "War" had lyrics taken from a speech by Haile Selassie. Selassie, a 20th century Ethiopian emperor, was seen as a spiritual leader in the Rastafarian movement. Marley supported the People's National Party (PNP). The rivals of this political party were supposedly behind the attempt to assassinate Marley in 1976.

Marley's 1977 album, 'Exodus', was part of the UK charts for more than a year. Its singles "Waiting in Vain" and "Jamming" were quite a hit. Marley performed in Jamaica at the One Love Peace Concert in 1978 and at the official independence ceremony of Zimbabwe in 1980.

Marley was awarded the 'Peace Medal of the Third World' by the United Nations in June 1978. He was also honored with the 'Jamaican Order of Merit' (the third highest honor of the nation) by the Jamaican government in February 1981. Posthumously, in February 2001, Marley was awarded the Grammy Lifetime Achievement Award. In the same year, Marley was inducted to the Hollywood Walk of Fame. He was also inducted to the Rock and Roll Hall of Fame in 1994. The album 'Catch a Fire' got inducted to the Grammy Hall of Fame in 2010.

Bob Marley changed his faith from Catholic to Rastafari in 1966. He married Alpharita Constantia Anderson (Rita) on 10th February, 1966. They had three children. Marley was diagnosed with malignant melanoma (an incurable skin cancer) in 1977. His health began to decline over the years. Marley died on 11th May, 1981 at Miami's Cedars of Lebanon Hospital. Jamaican Prime Minister Edward Seaga presided over his funeral service. He was buried at a chapel in Nine Mile. Marley's posthumous album 'Confrontation' was released in 1983. His statues were erected at Kingston, Jamaica and Banatski Sokolac, a village in Serbia. A movie, *Marley,* about the legendary musician, released in 2012.

DAVID BOWIE

BIRTH: January 8, 1947
Brixton, London, England

DEATH: January 10, 2016 (aged 69)
New York City, USA

Avid Bowie was an English singer, songwriter and actor. He is most known for his fictional character, "Ziggy Stardust". He was considered to be a musical chameleon of sorts.

David Bowie was born as David Robert Jones on 8th January, 1947, in Brixton, London. His mother, Margaret Mary "Peggy", worked as a waitress. His father, Haywood Stenton "John" Jones, was a promotions officer at a children's charity. His half-brother, Terry, nourished his interest in music. Terry was nine years elder to him, and he introduced Bowie to rock music and beat literature. Terry committed suicide in 1985. His death had quite an impact on Bowie and was the subject of Bowie's song "Jump They Say".

At the age of sixteen, Bowie graduated from Bromley Technical High School and started to work as a commercial artist. He also lead a group named Davy Jones and the Lower Third. In the 1960s, he changed his name to David Bowie to avoid confusion with the Monkees' David Jones. Bowie released his self-titled album in 1967. It did not gain much recognition. Bowie signed a deal with Mercury Records and got his first break with the 1969 single "Space Oddity". It was placed in the top five in the UK charts. This song was released in 1972 in the US and ranked number fifteen in the charts there.

His 1970 album 'The Man Who Sold the World' had the single, "All the Madmen". This song is also thought to be about his brother, Terry. His album 'Hunky Dory' was released in 1971. It contained songs in tribute to Andy Warhol and Bob Dylan. His 1972 album, 'The Rise and Fall of Ziggy Stardust and the Spiders from Mars' was in collaboration with The Spiders from Mars. It gained huge commercial success. It was based on a fictional rockstar, Ziggy Stardust, and his downfall. It ranked number five in the UK. He collaborated with Mick Jagger and Keith Richards for his 1973 album 'Aladdin Sane'. It contained songs like "The Jean Genie" and "Let's Spend the Night Together".

In 1973, his album 'Pin Ups' was released. It contained covers of songs by Pretty Things and Pink Floyd. His single "Fame", from 'Young Americans' topped the American charts. It was co-written by John Lennon. His 1983 album, 'Let's dance', contained singles such as "Modern Love" and "China Girl".

Bowie also acted in movies. He played a role in the 1976 movie *The Man Who Fell to Earth*. He has also acted in movies like *Merry Christmas, Mr. Lawrence, The Hunger* and *Jazzin' for Blue*

Jean. He appeared in Broadway's *The Elephant Man* around 1980.

Bowie collaborated with Reeves Gabrels, and Tony and Hunt Sales (collectively called the Tin Machine) for the albums 'Tin Machine' and 'Tin Machine II'. His 1993 album 'Black Tie White Noise' was dedicated to his wife, Iman, as a wedding gift. His albums in the 1990s include 'Outside', 'Earthling' and 'Hours'.

In 2013, Bowie's 'The Next Day' was released. It ranked number two on the Billboard charts. He released his final album, 'Blackstar', on 8th January, 2016 on his 69th birthday. Bowie won the Ivor Novello Special Award for Originality for the song "Space Oddity". He was posthumously awarded four Grammy Awards for his last album 'Blackstar', to honor his legacy. He has received the Brit Awards for 'Best British Male Artist' and 'Outstanding Contribution to Music'. On 17th January, 1996, Bowie was inducted to the Rock and Roll Hall of Fame. He was made a Commander of the Ordre des Arts et des Lettres in 1999 by the French government.

David Bowie got married to Mary Angela Barnett in 1970. They had a son in the following year. They separated in 1980. Bowie remarried the Somali model, Iman, in 1992. They had a daughter together.

Bowie passed away on 10th January, 2016, after battling cancer for eighteen months. David Bowie left a musical legacy of twenty-six albums. On 7th January, 2017, HBO released the documentary *David Bowie: The Last Five Years*. It contains backstage footage of his final tour and albums.

ELTON JOHN

BIRTH: March 25, 1947
Pinner, Middlesex, England

Elton Hercules John is a British singer, pianist and composer. In 1998, Elton John was knighted by Queen Elizabeth II. He has had seven consecutive US number one albums, including 'Tumbleweed Connection', 'Madman Across the Water', 'Honky Château', 'Don't Shoot Me I'm Only the Piano Player', 'Goodbye Yellow Brick Road', 'Caribou' and 'Rock of the Westies'. He has also had success in Broadway shows.

Elton John was born as Reginald Kenneth

Dwight on 25th March, 1947 at Pinner, Middlesex, England. His father, Stanley Dwight, was a squadron leader in the Royal Air Force. His mother, Sheila Eileen Dwight, was a homemaker. She brought records and introduced him to rock music. At the age of four, he used to play the piano on his own. He got a scholarship at the Royal Academy of Music at the age of eleven. In 1962, he joined a band named Bluesology with his friends. In 1962, he changed his name to Elton John to honor two of the band's members. John added Hercules as his middle name later later, and legally adopted the name Elton Hercules John in 1972.

In 1967, he collaborated with Bernie Taupin after answering an ad looking for a songwriter for Liberty Records. Their first song together was "Scarecrow". Both of the artists switched to DJM label in 1968 where they wrote songs for other artists. John and Taupin released their first album in 1969 called 'Empty Sky' which failed to garner much interest. It was Elton John's second album that gained him international success. Its single, "Your Song", was number four in the

US Billboard 200. His song "Crocodile Rock" was the first one to reach the US Billboard Hot 100. His other hit singles include "Daniel", "Bennie and the Jets" and "Island Girl".

In 1973, John founded The Rocket Record Company. In the 1970s, seven of his albums were number one on the music charts. John did a duet single, "Don't Go Breaking My Heart", with Kiki Dee in 1976. His 1989 single, "Sacrifice", was number one on the UK charts. It was his first solo UK hit. He wrote songs for the Disney movie *The Lion King* with Tim Rice in 1994. It was also adapted to Broadway in 1997. Elton John won his first Academy Award and a Golden Globe, in 1995, for "Can You Feel the Love Tonight" from the movie *The Lion King*.

In 1997, he performed "Candle in the Wind" at the funeral of Princess Diana. This song sold over thirty million records all around the world. It is one of the world's best-selling singles in Billboard history. It is platinum-certified in the United States. John and Tim

Rice collaborated again to give music to the stage musical *Elaborate Lives: The Legend of Aida*. It premiered on Broadway in 2000. It was awarded a Tony Award for Best Original Score.

Elton got his fifth UK number one with the song "Are You Ready for Love" in 2003. In 2016, he released his album 'Wonderful Crazy' and released 'Singing the Seventies' in 2019.

John has won five Grammy Awards as well as Brit Awards. In 1994, he was inducted to the Rock and Roll Hall of Fame. He was also inducted to the Songwriters Hall of Fame in 1992. He was honored with a star at the Hollywood Walk of Fame in 1975. In 2000, The National Academy of Recording Arts and Science credited John's charity work by honoring him as Person of the Year. *Rolling Stone* magazine included John Elton in the 49th position in the list of '100 Greatest Artists of All Time'. He received his first Brits Icon Award in 2013.

In the 1980s, John Elton was involved in campaigns associated with AIDS awareness. All the profits from his 1986 single "That's What Friends Are For" were donated to the American Foundation for AIDS Research. This song was a joint venture with Dionne Warwick, Gladys Knight and Stevie Wonder. The song also won a Grammy Award for 'Best Pop Performance by a Duo or Group with Vocals'. John also founded his charitable foundation, the Elton John AIDS Foundation, in 1992. John also supports arts organizations such as the Globe Theatre and the Royal Academy of Music.

John married Renate Blauel in 1984. They got a divorce four years later in 1988. He came out as homosexual in 1988, and started dating David Furnish in 1993. The Civil Partnership Act was enforced in 2005. This couple was amongst the first to get a civil partnership in the UK. They had two children by surrogacy. On 21st December, 2014, John and Fisher got married, as gay marriage was announced to be lawful in Britain.

ELVIS PRESLEY

BIRTH: January 8, 1935
Tupelo, Mississippi, USA

DEATH: August 16, 1977
Memphis, Tennessee, USA

Elvis Aaron Presley was an American singer and actor. He is called the "King of Rock and Roll". In 1986, he was one of the first people to be inducted to the Rock and Roll Hall of Fame.

Elvis Presley was born to Vernon and Gladys Presley on 8th January, 1935. He was born in Tupelo, Mississippi.

When Elvis was thirteen years old, their family moved to Memphis, Tennessee. He studied at Humes High School. Presley won a talent show in his school. He graduated in the year 1953. The factors influencing him at the time were the country and pop music of the time, and the all-night gospel music he heard at church.

Country singers like Ted Daffan, Ernest Tubb and Jake Hess were an inspiration for Presley. In 1954, he recorded at Sun Records Label. Sun's boss, Sam Phillips made him re-record in 1954. Presley sang Arthur Crudup's "That's All Right" with local musicians—Scotty Moore playing the guitar and Bill Black as the bassist. This song aired three days later and gained quite some popularity. They started doing concerts from then on.

Elvis Presley got his record deal with RCA in 1955 with the help of his manager, Colonel Tom Parker. On 23rd March of the next year, his self-titled album was released. His first hit, "Heartbreak Heart" was from this album. This song topped the pop charts for seven weeks. In

1956, Elvis also signed a movie contract with Paramount Pictures. His film *Love Me Tender* was released in the same year; it was a box office hit.

Elvis Presley was inducted to the US Army in 1958. He was stationed at Germany. He gave his services to the army for two years and retired from the Third Armored Division with the rank of sergeant.

Presley's comeback album, 'Elvis is Back' came out in April 1960. The next album, 'Something for Everybody' was released in 1961. Presley starred in Norman Taurog's musical comedy G.I. Blues in 1960. He also gave the soundtrack for this movie. Next he starred in *Blue Hawaii, Girls! Girls! Girls!* and *Viva Las Vegas*. On 3rd December, 1968, Elvis Presley appeared in his first TV special which was referred to as his "'68 Comeback Special". His album, 'From Elvis in Memphis' came out the next year. His number one hit single "Suspicious Minds" was from this album.

His 1970 single, 'The Wonder of You' topped the UK and US charts. He has had three television specials, *Elvis* in 1968, *Elvis: Aloha from Hawaii, Via Satellite* in 1973, and *Elvis in Concert* in 1977.

His health began to deteriorate in 1973 while he continued to manage his hectic touring schedule.

Elvis sold millions of records all over the world. He was nominated for fourteen Grammy Awards and won three times. 'How Great Thou Art', 'He touched Me' and his Memphis concert of the song "How Great Thou Art", all received Grammy Awards. He was also honoured with the Lifetime Achievement Award in 1971. Elvis Presley's recordings are also included in the NARAS Hall of Fame. He was named as one of the 'Ten Outstanding Young Men of the Nation for 1970' by the United States Junior Chamber of Commerce. Elvis Presley was inducted to the Rock and Roll Hall of Fame in 1986. He was also inducted to the Gospel Music Hall of Fame in 2001, the Rockabilly Hall of Fame in 2007, and the Country Music Hall of Fame in 1998. He was awarded the American Music Awards' Award of Merit in 1987.

He was credited with 146.5 million certified album sales in the US by Recording Industry Association of America (RIAA) in 2018.

While in the military in Germany, Presley met Priscilla Beaulieu. They got married in 1967. They had a daughter, Lisa Marie, in 1968. In 1973, they divorced, and Priscilla got the custody of Lisa Marie. Lisa Marie became a singer later in her life.

On 16th August, 1977, Elvis Presley died of heart failure. Presley was buried at the Graceland estate. Since the 1980s, Presley's home, Graceland, has been open to the public. It attracts tourist and fans. In 2006, this place was declared as a National Historic Landmark.

FREDDIE MERCURY

BIRTH: September 5, 1946
Stone Town, Zanzibar

DEATH: November 24, 1991
Kensington, London, England

Freddie Mercury was a rock singer and songwriter of the British rock band, Queen. Queen is known for their mock operatic masterpiece, "Bohemian Rhapsody". Mercury is popularly known for his vocal abilities.

Freddie Mercury was born as Farrokh Bulsara on 5th September, 1946. He was born in the East African island of Zanzibar, Tanzania. He was born in a Parsi family to Bomi and Jer Bulsara. He had a younger sibling, Kashmira.

Mercury attended St Peter's Boarding School in Panchgani, Maharashtra, India. At the age of seven, Mercury began to learn the piano. He created a band called The Hectics in 1958. They would play songs by Little Richard and Cliff Richard. In 1964, the Bulsara family shifted to Feltham, England. Mercury attended Ealing Technical College and School of Art (now part of the University of West London) to study art and graphic design. He graduated in 1969. After graduation, he survived by selling old clothes at London's Kensington Market and working at Heathrow Airport. He joined several bands during this time, including Ibex and Sour Milk Sea.

In 1970, Mercury became friends with drummer Roger Taylor and guitarist Brian May. They had a band named Smile. When the lead singer of the group left, Mercury filled in for him. The group's name was changed to "Queen", and he officially named himself Freddie Mercury. In 1971, bassist John Deacon joined the band.

They released their first album, 'Queen', in 1973 and 'Queen II' in 1974. But both of these albums were unsuccessful despite the quality of music. It was their third release, 'Sheer Heart Attack' that popularized them. Its single "Killer Queen" was number two on the UK charts and number twelve in the US. Their 1975 album, 'A Night at the Opera' gave them one of their biggest hits, "Bohemian Rhapsody". It was a seven-minute rock operetta and topped the British singles charts for nine weeks. Their single, "We are the Champions" was part of the 1977 album 'News of the World'. It was in the Top 10 Hits charts in the US.

Queen is also famous for its live performances. On 13th July, 1985, they did a 'Live Aid' concert at London's Wembley Stadium. It was organized by singer and activist Bob Geldof and songwriter Midge Ure to raise funds for victims of famine in Ethiopia. Their song "One Vision" is speculated to be inspired from this event.

Mercury released his first solo album, 'Mr. Bad Guy', in 1985. It had eleven songs written by

Mercury. The next year, he also collaborated with Spanish Soprano singer, Montserrat Caballe for his album, 'Barcelona'. It contained songs in Spanish, Japanese and English.

In 1992, he was awarded the Brit Award for Outstanding Contribution to British Music. Mercury, along with his bandmates, was inducted to the Rock and Roll Hall of Fame in 2001, and the Songwriters Hall of Fame in 2003. He was also inducted to the UK Music Hall of Fame in 2004. The Guinness Book of World Records has recognized "Bohemian Rhapsody" and "We are the Champions" as the greatest songs of all time. These songs also belong to the Grammy Hall of Fame.

Mercury was in a six-year-long relationship with Mary Austin, until 1976. They lived together in West Kingston, London. In the 1980s, Mercury was supposedly in a relationship with the Austrian actor, Barbara Valentin.

On 24th November, 1991, Mercury passed away due to bronchopneumonia caused by HIV/AIDS. He had publicly announced that he had this disease just one day before. Jim Hutton later revealed that Mercury had been diagnosed in 1987. His funeral was held three days later in Parsi tradition. His body was buried at Kensal Green Cemetery in West London.

In 1995, Queen's album 'Made in Heaven' was released. It contained songs recorded by Mercury before his death. BBC named him in the list of the '100 Greatest Britons'. He was also recognized by *Rolling Stone* magazine in the list of 'Top 100 Singers of All Time'. The remaining members of Queen and Jim Beach, their manager, founded The Mercury Phoenix Trust in 1992. It organized concerts to raise funds for HIV/AIDS. Charles Messina wrote a monodrama *Mercury: The Afterlife and Times of a Rock God* in his honor. It was first performed in 1997. In 1996, a bronze statue of Freddie Mercury was placed by the waterfront in Montreux, Switzerland.

JAMES BROWN

BIRTH: May 3, 1933
Barnwell, South Carolina, USA

DEATH:December 25, 2006
Atlanta, Georgia, USA

James Joe Brown, Jr. was an African-American singer, songwriter and dancer. He is considered to be the inventor of funk music. He is also called the "Godfather of Soul".

James Brown was born to James Joe, Sr. and Susie Brown on 3rd May, 1933. His mother left the family when he was just four years old. Brown moved to Augusta, Georgia to live with his Aunt Honey. He lived in poverty during the Great Depression. He worked odd jobs such as shining shoes and washing cars. Brown was dismissed from school at the age of twelve due to "insufficient clothes". He used to sing in the church choir. His neighbors taught him to play the drums, guitar and piano. He got arrested at the age of fifteen for stealing cars. In prison, he met Bobby Byrd, an aspiring R&B singer and pianist.

He was released from prison in less than four years. For two years he played sports such as boxing. He was also a semi-professional baseball player. In 1955, Bobby Byrd asked Brown to join his R&B vocal group, The Gospel Starlighters. It was renamed to The Famous Flames. They moved to Macon, Georgia and performed at nightclubs.

The Famous Flames played their demo tape of the song "Please, Please, Please" for King Records' Ralph Bass who immediately signed them on in 1956. Their first single "Please, Please, Please" hit the R&B charts at number six. It sold about a million copies. In 1958, Brown moved to New

York to keep his creative spark alive, while also working with The Flames, and released the song, "Try Me". It became the number one song on R&B charts. It also acquired a place in the Hot 100 Singles charts. His other major hits include "Lost Someone", "Night Train" and "Prisoner of Love".

He performed many shows in the 1950s and 60s. He used to perform five to six nights a week. This work ethic earned him the title of "The Hardest-Working Man in Show Business". In 1963, he released a live concert album recorded at the Apollo Theatre. It was called 'Live at the Apollo'. It acquired the number two position on the pop charts. It is seen as Brown's greatest commercial success and stayed on the charts for sixty -six weeks.

His 1966 song, "Papa's Got a Brand New Bag", belonged to the new music genre of funk. This genre became the precursor to hip-hop music. His song "Cold Sweat" is also considered to be a pure funk song. In 1964, his live album 'Pure Dynamite! Live at the Royale' ranked in the pop charts for twenty-two weeks.

James Brown was also referred to as "Soul Brother No.1". He created music in support of the Black Nationalist movements. His songs "Say It Loud: I'm Black and I'm Proud" and "I Don't Want Nobody to Give Me Nothin" reflect his support. He also released an educational song in 1966 called "Don't be a Drop-out".

He acted in the 1980 movie, *The Blues Brothers*. In 1985, he released a song called "Living in America". It was featured in the movie *Rocky IV*. It was his first million-selling hit in thirteen years. He received a Grammy for 'Best R&B Performance by a Male Artist' for this song in 1986.

In February 1992, he was given the Lifetime Achievement Award at the Grammy Awards. He was honored with the BET Lifetime Achievement Award in 2003. Brown was one of the first singers to be inducted to the Rock and Roll Hall of Fame on its inauguration in 1986.

James Brown was married four times. His last marriage was with Tomi Rae Hynie, in 2001. However, since she was legally married to someone else, this marriage was not valid under South Carolina laws. Brown has several children from these marriages.

James Brown passed away on 25th December, 2006, due to congestive heart failure caused by pneumonia. He was 73 years old.

Brown's works have had a major role in shaping the cultural history of America. In his memoirs, he wrote, "Others may have followed in my wake, but I was the one who turned racist minstrelsy into black soul—and by doing so, became a cultural force." Brown has also influenced artists such as Michael Jackson, Mick Jagger and Jay-Z. The Godfather of Soul carries his legacy from beyond the grave.

JIMI HENDRIX

BIRTH: November 27, 1942
Seattle, Washington, USA

DEATH: September 18, 1970 (aged 27)
Kensington, London, England

Jimi Hendrix was an African-American guitarist, singer and songwriter. He is one of the greatest guitarists of all times.

Jimi Hendrix was born as Johnny Allen Hendrix on 27th November, 1942. His father, Al Hendrix, was a jazz dancer and worked many other jobs. His mother was Lucille Jeter. He was the eldest of five children. His father changed Johnny's name to James Marshal in 1946. His parents got a divorce in 1951. Hendrix was nine years old at that time. His father got custody of the children. Lucille Jeter died on 2nd February, 1958. His father and paternal grandmother raised Hendrix.

Hendrix's interest in music developed at an early age. He would use the broom as a guitar or a one-string ukulele. His father got him his first acoustic guitar at the age of twelve. In 1956, he got his first electric guitar—a white Supro Ozark. As he was left-handed, he had to turn the guitar in the opposite direction while playing. This gave him his unique performing style. He liked the blues, and rock and roll music. He was also influenced by artists such as B.B. King, Muddy Waters, Albert King, and Elmore James. Blues guitarists Steve Cropper and Curtis Mayfield also inspired his style of music.

The Velvetones was the first formal band that he played in. He then joined the band the Rocking Kings. Hendrix dropped out of Garfield

High School in 1959. He worked odd jobs while pursuing his career in music.

Hendrix joined the army at the age of seventeen in order to avoid a jail sentence. He was stationed in Fort Campbell, Kentucky. He had volunteered as a paratrooper. The following year, Hendrix got discharged from the army due to an injury caused while jumping from a parachute.

Hendrix met Billy Cox (a bass player) during the service. They formed a band called The King Casuals. They used to perform at clubs in Nashville, Tennessee. After the service, Jimmy started working under the name Jimmy James. He worked as a backup for B.B. King, Little Richard, Sam Cooke, and the Isle Brothers. In 1966, he got a contract with Curtis Knight's manager, and formed his group, Jimmy James and the Blue Flames.

Hendrix was spotted by Bryan Chandler, bass player of British rock band, The Animals, in 1964. Chandler made Hendrix move to London and start a band. Hendrix started The Jimi Hendrix Experience in 1966 with Noel

Redding as the bassist and John "Mitch" Mitchell as the drummer.

The band's first single, "Hey Joe", was released in 1967. It became a huge hit and was performed on a stage show in London. This was followed with hits such as "Purple Haze" and "The Wind Cries Mary". Their first album called 'Are you Experienced?' released in 1967. Their performance at the Monterey Pop Festival created a ripple amongst their audiences. Hendrix experimented with his song writing skills in the second album, 'Axis: Bold as Love', in 1967. Their 1969 album, 'Electric Ladyland', contained the hit song "All Along the Watchtower". This song was written by Bob Dylan. The band's most memorable performance includes playing "the Star-Spangled Banner" at the Woodstock festival in New York in 1969. The band broke up the same year due to a contractual disagreement between Hendrix and Ed Chaplin.

Hendrix formed a group with his old friends, Billy Cox and Buddy Miles. They created the live album 'Band of Gypsys' in 1970 before Miles left the group.

Jimi Hendrix was inducted to the Rock and Roll Hall of Fame in 1992. The same year, he was posthumously awarded the Grammy Award for Lifetime Achievement. In 1993, Eric Clapton recorded his version of Hendrix's "Stone Free" for an album called 'Stone Free: A Tribute to Jimi Hendrix'. Many rock, blues, rap artists created versions of his songs for this album. James Allen Hendrix published a biography based on the family life of Jimi Hendrix, called *My Son Jimi*.

In 2005, Hendrix was inducted to the UK Music Hall of Fame. He is one of the first people who was inducted to the Native American Music Hall of Fame. He got a star on the Hollywood Walk of Fame in 1994.

Hendrix passed away on 18th September, 1970 in London, because of an overdose of sleeping pills. He was 27 years old.

JOHN LENNON

BIRTH: October 9, 1940
Liverpool, England

DEATH: December 8, 1980
New York, USA

John Lennon was a British musician. He was a singer, songwriter and a graphic artist. He led The Beatles, a British rock band.

John Winston Ono Lennon was born in Liverpool, England, during a German air raid in World War II. His parents were separated when he was five years old. John was brought up by his maternal aunt, Mimi

Smith, at Woolton in Liverpool. His mother, Julia, had taught him to play the banjo and the piano. She bought him his first guitar. She died in a car accident in July 1958.

In the September of 1956, at the age of sixteen, John Lennon started his skiffle band. It was named The Quarrymen, after Lennon's school, the Quarry Bank High School. Lennon met Paul McCartney in July 1957 in a church fête. He soon joined Lennon's band. In the following year, Paul introduced Lennon to George Harrison who also became a member of the band, along with his friend from art school, Stuart Sutcliffe. Pete Best joined their band as a drummer in 1960.

Their first recording was Buddy Holly's "That'll Be the Day" in 1958. They got their first break when Brian Epstein saw them perform at Liverpool's Cavern Club in 1961. With his help, they signed a contract with the EMI Group, and George Martin became their producer. Ringo Starr (Richard Starkey) replaced Pete Best as the drummer of the band soon after.

The Beatles' first single was "Love Me Do". It was

released in October 1962. It hit the seventeenth position on the British charts. Their second single, "Please Please Me", came second on the British charts.

They were the first band to break out big in the US after their appearance on *The Ed Sullivan Show* in 1964. Their first film, *A Hard Day's Night*, also came out in 1964. In 1965, their second film, *Help!*, was released. The Beatles were made Members of the Order of the British Empire by Queen Elizabeth II in June 1965. In August of the same year, they gave a performance in front of approximately 56,000 fans at New York's Shea Stadium. It was a new record for the largest audience in musical history. Their album 'Rubber Soul' came out the same year. Their 1964 song "I Want to Hold Your Hand" sold millions of copies. They had a US tour in the same year. With their increasing popularity and support, the word "Beatlemania" began to be used commonly.

On 27th August, 1967, Brian Epstein passed away. The Beatles were quite affected by this news. Hence, their 1967 *Magical Mystery Tour* did not gain much commercial success.

In the September of 1969, John Lennon left the band. McCartney left the group in April of the next year.

Lennon released his solo album titled 'John Lennon/Plastic Ono Band' in 1970. In 1971, his album 'Imagine' was also released. In the September of 1972, Lennon and Yoko Ono moved to the US, but shortly after, Lennon was made to leave the country for his protests against the Vietnam War. His song "Give Peace a Chance" is considered an anti-war song for the same motive. However, after a long struggle, Lennon received permanentcitizenshipin1976. Lennonalsocollaborated with David Bowie and Elton John during this period. His album 'Double Fantasy' was released in 1980. The single "(Just Like) Starting Over" became a major hit.

Lennon was posthumously inducted to the Songwriters Hall of Fame in 1987 and Rock and Roll Hall of Fame in 1994. John Lennon and Paul McCartney, together, won a Grammy for their song "Michelle" at the 10th Grammy Awards held in 1967.

The Beatles were awarded the Grammy Lifetime Achievement award in 2014. They have had 45 Gold albums in the United States. In 1977, they were honored with The Brit Award for 'Best British Group'. In 1971, they won the Academy Award for 'Best Music' for the documentary *Let It Be*.

John Lennon married Cynthia Powell in the year 1962, when he was twenty-one years old. They had a son named Julian. They got divorced in 1968. A year later, he married Yoko Ono, whom he had met at the Indica gallery in 1966. They married in the March of 1969. They also had a son together, named Sean in 1975.

On 8th December, 1980, Lennon was shot by Mark David Chapman while in Dakota, New York. Shortly after, Lennon was pronounced dead at the Roosevelt Hospital. He was cremated at the Ferncliff Cemetery in Hartsdale, New York. His ashes were scattered at the New York Central Park by his wife.

JOHANN SEBASTIAN BACH

BIRTH: March 31, 1685
Eisenach, Thuringia, Germany

DEATH: July 28, 1750
Leipzig, Germany

Johann Sebastian Bach was a German composer and a musician of the Baroque period. His most famous compositions include "Brandenburg Concertos", "Mass in B Minor", "The Well-Tempered Clavier" and "Goldberg Variations".

Johann Sebastian was born to Johann Ambrosius and Maria Elizabeth Lämmerhirt Bach on 31st March,

1685. His father was a town musician and a church organist in Eisenach. Both his parents passed away in 1695.

His elder brother, Johann Christoph took two of his younger brothers under his care. Johann Sebastian (ten years old) and Johann Jacob Bach (thirteen years old) moved to Ohrdruf, Germany with him. Johann Christoph was an organist at St Michael's Church.

Johann Sebastian Bach was appointed as Mettenchor at the school at Michaelskirche. As his voice changed, he started focusing on playing the violin and harpsichord. It's believed that while studying church music in the school library, Bach might have heard George Bohm who was an organist of the Johanniskirche, and that Böhm heavily influenced him. Bach went to Lubeck to listen to organist Johann Adam Reinken play. Bach became an organist at the Church of St Blaise in Mühlhausen in 1707. His famous composition from that time includes the cantata "Gottes Zeit ist die allerbeste Zeit", also called "Actus Tragicus".

In 1708, Bach found a position as the court organist of Duke Wilhelm Ernst and went back to Weimar. He wrote, "Toccata and Fugue in D minor" and the cantata "Herz und Mund und Tat" ("Heart and Mouth and Deed") during this time.

Bach accepted the position of Kapellmeister for Prince Leopold of Köthen in 1717. Bach journeyed to Köthen where he focused on instrumental music and created some of his greatest works.

Bach composed the "Brandenburg Concertos" in 1721, in honor of the Duke of Brandenburg. It is considered one of the best compositions of the era. He also completed the first book of "Well-Tempered Clavier" around this time. In 1723, he became the new organist for the St Thomas Church in Leipzig. He had to supply music to four churches as the director of church music for the city. He acquired the directorship of the Collegium Musicum in 1729. It was a secular musical ensemble of professional and amateur musicians.

His secular compositions comprised of musical interpretations of the Bible. One of the examples being his "Passions". The "St Matthew Passion" is based on the stories of chapters 26 and 27 of the Gospel of Matthew.

Bach became a court composer in Saxony in 1733. Bach's 'The Goldberg Variations' was published in 1741. It was named after Johann Gottlieb Goldberg. Bach joined the Correspondierende Societät der musicalischen Wissenschaften (Corresponding Society of the Musical Sciences) founded by his former pupil Lorenz Christoph Mizler Von Koloff in 1747. He also performed for the King of Prussia, Frederick the Great, in the same year. He composed a set of fugues, "Musical Offerings" for the Prussian King. His health and eyesight began to decline around this time.

His major work, "Mass in B-Major" was completed around 1749. The short verses, Kyrie and Gloria, were supposedly written for the Protestant court services in Dresden. His last work, "The Art of the Fugue", was left incomplete as he passed away the next year. It was still published in 1751. Bach became completely blind four months before his death due to an eye operation.

Bach married twice and his last marriage was to Anna Magdalena Wilcke, a court singer. He had four children from his first marriage and six from his second. Many of Bach's children became renowned singers.

Bach passed away on 28th July, 1750, due to a stroke. He died in Leipzig, at the age of sixty-five. During his lifetime, Bach wasn't paid adequately. Neither was he well appreciated for his talent. In 1829, German composer Felix Mendelssohn reintroduced Bach's "St Matthew Passion". This brought new popularity to Bach. Pablo Casals also helped in popularizing Bach's "Cello Suites". Bach is referred to as one of the best composers of the Baroque period and remains a major figure amongst classical musicians.

KURT COBAIN

BIRTH: February 20, 1967
Aberdeen, Washington, USA

DEATH: April 5, 1994
Seattle, Washington, USA

Kurt Donald Cobain was an American rock musician. He was the singer, guitarist and songwriter of Nirvana, an American grunge band. Cobain is the most popular rock legend of the 1990s.

Cobain was born on 20th February, 1967 in Aberdeen, Washington. He was nine years old when his parents separated.

He started living with his father and his new family. His behavior turned increasingly bitter towards his parents and so he was moved to a family friend's house. They were devout Christians and Cobain felt drawn to the religion for a short while. He began to live with his mother in his second year of high school. Cobain left Aberdeen High School just two weeks before his graduation.

He came to be friends with Buzz Osbourne, the founding member of the local punk rock band, Melvins, in the mid-1980s. At the Melvins' practice space, Cobain met Krist Novoselic. They formed a band together in 1987.

In 1988, the band decided upon the name "Nirvana". They released their first single "Love Buzz" in 1988, through an independent record label, Sub Pop Records. The following year, they released their first album 'Bleach'. It had a punk base with heavy metal sounds. Their first drummer was Aaron Burckhard. He was replaced by Chad Channing in 1988. In 1990, the band toured with Sonic Youth. Dave Grohl became a part of the band at this time. He replaced Channing as Cobain became unhappy with Channing's style. Nirvana joined Geffen Records in 1991. Their album 'Nevermind' was released in the same year. It was the first alternative rock album to gain popular success; it was actually their greatest success as a band. Its single, "Smells like Teen Spirit", topped the music charts. Cobain was declared the best songwriter of the generation, a title he struggled to accept. Cobain was just 24 years old then.

In the September of 1993, their album 'In Utero' came out, it shot to the number one spot on music charts. Its singles, "Radio Friendly Unit Shifter" and "Heart Shaped-Box", were quite a hit. In the fall of 1993 they performed for MTV's Unplugged in New York City.

In 2003, David Fricke of *Rolling Stone* honored Cobain as the twelfth greatest guitarist of all time. MTV ranked him seventh in their list of '22 Greatest Voices in Music'. Cobain was inducted to the Rock and Roll Hall of Fame in 2014, along with Nirvana members, Novoselic and Dave

Grohl. Michael Azerrad published a book in 1993, called *Come As You Are: The Story of Nirvana.*

Kurt Cobain met Courtney Love at a Portland Nightclub in 1989. Courtney Love was the lead singer and guitarist of the band, Hole. They got married in February 1992 and in the same year their daughter, Frances Bean Cobain, was born.

On 8th April, 1994, an electrician found Cobain's dead body at his Lake Washington Boulevard home. He had reportedly shot himself on 5th April, 1994. He was 27 years old. He continues to be remembered amongst the music legends. Cobain was cremated and his remains scattered in Wishkah River, Washington. On his death anniversary, many of his fans visit Viretta Park, near his Lake Washington home, to pay tribute. In 2004, the Kurt Cobain Memorial Committee put up a sign that read "Come As You Are" at Aberdeen, Washington, in his honor. The committee was created in May 2004 to honor Cobain.

He was the topic of many posthumous works. The book *Heavier than Heaven: A Biography of*

Kurt Cobain by Charles R. Cross was published in 2001. Documentaries based on him include *Kurt and Courtney* and *Kurt Cobain: Montage of Heck.*

Nirvana released their *Unplugged* session after Cobain's death. It topped the album charts. On October 1, 1996, the band released a collection of songs, 'From the Muddy Banks of the Wishkah'. It was also a commercial success. 'Nirvana', 'With the Lights Out' and 'Silver: The Best of the Box' were other albums released by Grohl, Novoselic and Love, post Cobain's death.

LOUIS ARMSTRONG

BIRTH: August 4, 1901
New Orleans, Louisiana, USA

DEATH: July 6, 1971
Queens, New York, USA

Louis Daniel Armstrong was an African-American jazz trumpeter and singer. He was popularly referred to as "Satchmo", "Pops" and "Ambassador Satch".

He was born on 4th August, 1901 in the "Battlefield" area of New Orleans, Louisiana. His father, Willie Armstrong, was a turpentine worker.

His father left them shortly after his birth. He used to live with his maternal grandmother for long periods of time. Armstrong left school in the fifth grade to start earning. He used to sing in the streets as a child. He also worked with a Jewish family named the Karnofskys. There, his work was to collect junk and sell coal.

In 1913, he was sent to Colored Waif's Home for Boys, a home for juvenile delinquents. There, he learned to play the cornet and found his passion for music. He learned music from several mentors, including Buddy Petit, Kid Ory and Joe "King" Oliver, one of the finest cornet players whom he befriended.

In 1918, Armstrong took Oliver's position in Kid Ory's band. It was the most popular jazz band in New Orleans. He moved to Chicago in 1922 and became a part of King Oliver's Creole Jazz Band. His first recordings with the band include "Chimes Blues" and "Tears". Armstrong joined Fletcher Henderson's Orchestra in New York City in 1924, in search of further fame. It was the top African-American dance band at the time. He returned to Chicago a year later and composed his most significant works with Okeh Records, namely 'Louis Armstrong and His Hot Five'. From 1925 to 1928, Armstrong recorded about sixty jazz records with the Hot Five, which later became the Hot Seven. Armstrong also recorded with pianist Earl Hines and drummer Zutty Singleton in 1928. They composed "Weather Bird" and "West End Blues".

Armstrong had amassed immense popularity by 1930. He bagged a role in the Broadway production of *Hot Chocolates* directed by Leonard Harper in 1929. In 1936, he played the lead role in the movie, *Pennies from Heaven*. In the following year, he hosted a radio show, *'The Fleischmann's Yeast Hour'* for twelve weeks. Thus, he became amongst the first African-Americans to host a nationally sponsored broadcast.

Some of his greatest recordings are "Swing That Music", "Jubilee" and "Struttin' with Some

Barbecue". He toured and performed in Europe, Africa and Asia in the 1950s. CBS reporter Edward R. Murrow and his crew covered his events and created a documentary named *Satchmo the Great*, in 1957. In the December of 1964, his title for a Broadway show, "Hello, Dolly" topped the music charts. He also toured the Communist countries of East Berlin and Czechoslovakia in 1965. He composed a ballad called "What a Wonderful World" in 1967, which hit the number one spot in the UK Singles charts.

The Academy of Recording Arts and Science posthumously honored Louis Armstrong with the Grammy Lifetime Achievement Award in 1972. Armstrong's recordings were inducted to the Grammy Hall of Fame. Armstrong's "West End Blues" was a part of the '500 Songs that Shaped Rock and Roll' by the Rock and Roll Hall of Fame. He got a star on the Hollywood Walk of Fame in 1960. The US Post Office issued a Louis Armstrong postage stamp in 1995. He was also inducted to the DownBeat Jazz Hall of Fame in 1952.

He was married four times. His last marriage was to singer Lucille Wilson in 1942. Armstrong never had a child from any of his marriages.

However, in 2012, Sharon Preston claimed to be his biological daughter as she possessed letters written by the singer. Armstrong had also paid for her education and home. This reveals that Armstrong believed Sharon to be his daughter.

Armstrong's health began to deteriorate around the 1960s. He started suffering from heart problems. On 6th July, 1971, he died in his sleep at his home in Queens, New York. He passed away month before his seventieth birthday.

In 1977, Armstrong's home in Corona, Queens, was declared a National Historic Landmark. His home became the Louis Armstrong House Museum. The autobiographies published by Armstrong are *Swing That Music and Satchmo: My Life in New Orleans*. Armstrong was one of the greatest musicians of the 20th century. His contribution, both as a trumpeter

LUDWIG VAN BEETHOVEN

BIRTH: c. 1770
Bonn, Germany

DEATH: March 26, 1827 (aged 56)
Vienna, Austria

Ludwig van Beethoven was a composer and musician who connected the Classical and Romantic ages of Western music.

Beethoven was born in Bonn in the Electorate of Cologne, a principality of the Holy Roman Empire. Beethoven was the eldest child of Johann Van Beethoven and Maria Magdalena Keverich.

His father was a court musician.

Beethoven belonged to a musical family. His grandfather was a singer in the choir of the Archbishop Elector of Cologne, and later he became the Kapellmeister. Ludwig learned the violin and clavier from his father.

Ludwig van Beethoven's first recital took place in 1778. He attended the Latin grade school, Tirocinium. He left his education at the age of eleven, in order to pursue music. He went on to study music under Christian Gottlob Neefe. He used to fill Neefe's position as a church organist in his absence. At twelve years of age, Beethoven created his first composition, 'Nine Variations on a March by Dressler', a set of piano variations.

Ludwig Beethoven left for Vienna, Austria in the year 1787. It is assumed that he wanted to make Wolfgang Amadeus Mozart his guide. However, he had to come back to Bonn due to the ailing health of his mother who died the same year.

Beethoven was given the honor of composing a musical memorial for the demise of the Holy Roman Emperor, Joseph II, in 1790. His composition, "Cantata on the Death of Emperor Joseph II" was found a century later. After the demise of his father, Beethoven went back to Vienna. Here, he learned music under the guidance of Joseph Haydn. He acquired the reputation of a piano virtuoso while in Vienna.

In 1795, Beethoven published his first mature work. It was a series of three piano trios called "Opus 1, Three Trios for Piano, Violin, and Cello". It was supposedly dedicated to his patron, Prince Lichnowsky. He completed his work "Op 18", containing his first six quartets, in 1799. Beethoven's ballet, 'The Creatures of Prometheus' was first performed in 1801. It gained immense popularity.

In 1801, at the age of 30, Beethoven addressed a letter to a friend, Franz Wegeler, saying, "For the last three years, my hearing has grown steadily weaker." He further described his feelings about his deafness, "I must confess that I lead a miserable life. For almost two years, I have ceased to attend any social functions, just because I find it impossible to say to people: I am deaf. If I had any other profession, I might be able to cope with my infirmity; but in my profession it is a terrible handicap." He was advised by his doctor to live in Heiligenstadt, a small town outside Vienna. He wrote his famous Heiligenstadt Testament, a letter to his brothers, in 1802.

Even with his increasing deafness, Beethoven continued to compose at an alarming rate. The years from 1803 to 1812 are considered to be his "heroic" period. During this time, he was immersed in producing numerous piano sonatas, symphonies, string sonatas, string quartets, solo concerti, piano variations, overtures, trios, sextets, and many songs. He also composed an opera, 'Fidelio'. It is his only opera composition.

In May 1799, Beethoven taught music to

the daughters of the Hungarian Count Graf von Brunsvik. He was supposedly attracted to the younger daughter, Josephine. However, they did not get married, instead Josephine later married Graf von Deym. When Deym died in 1804, Beethoven and Josephine's relationship supposedly intensified. It is suggested that she might be Beethoven's "Immortal Beloved". In the July of 1812, Beethoven addressed two love letters to confess his feelings to his "immortal beloved". After his death, three letters were found from his locker, which either might never have been sent, or were sent but returned. Till date, the identity of Beethoven's "Immortal Beloved" remains a mystery.

Ludwig van Beethoven died on March 26, 1827, at the age of fifty-six. He died from cirrhosis of the liver in Vienna.

MADONNA

BIRTH: August 16, 1958
Bay City, Michigan, USA

adonna Louise Ciccone is an American singer,
performer and actor. She is called "The Queen
of Pop". She is known for reinventing her style of
music and image in the music industry.

Madonna was born to Silvio Ciccone
and Madonna Fortin on 16th August, 1958,
in Michigan, United States. Her father was
an engineer. Madonna is the third child
of her parents; she has seven siblings. The
Ciccone family belonged to the Catholic faith.
After her mother's death, her father remarried.

Madonna was a hard-working and disciplined student. She graduated early and in 1976, got accepted to the University of Michigan, where she studied dance for two years. Madonna moved to New York after dropping out of the University to pursue a career in dance. She did odd jobs to pay her rent. The following year, she attended Alvin Ailey's American Dance Theatre.

Madonna played drums in and sang for a number of New York-based groups, including Emmy, the Millionaires, and the Breakfast Club. Madonna also played a part in the movie *A Certain Sacrifice* in 1979.

Madonna signed with Sire Records. Her first single, "Everybody" from 1982, topped the dance charts. In 1983, her first album, 'Madonna' was released, which gradually gained success. It was her second album, 'Like a Virgin', which gave her international recognition. It sold over ten million copies. The title track of this album was number one on the Billboard Hot 100 Charts for six weeks.

In 1985, she starred in the film *Desperately*

Seeking Susan. She also sang "Into the Grove" for this movie. She sang "Crazy for You" the same year, for the movie *Vision Quest*, which also hit the number one spot in the Billboard Hot 100 Category. She also went on her first concert tour, called 'The Virgin Tour', the same year.

In 1986, her album 'True Blue' came out. It contained the hit singles "Papa Don't Preach", "True Blue" and "Live to Tell". In 1990, she released her compilation album, 'The Immaculate Collection'.

Madonna co-founded Maverick records in association with the Warner music group in 1992. In 1996, she played Eva Peron in the musical drama *Evita* and received the Golden Globe for Best Actress (Musical or Comedy) for this performance, in 1997.

Madonna is also associated with production companies and fashion lines. These include Hard Candy Fitness, Truth or Dare by Madonna, and Material Girl.

She received her first Grammy award in 1991

for 'Madonna—Blond Ambition World Tour Live' in the category of 'Best Music Video, Long Form'. She has won six more Grammy Awards since then. Madonna is credited with over sixteen Guinness World Records. Her world records include 'Highest grossing music tour by a female artist', 'Most US top 40 singles entries by a female artist', 'Most No.1 albums by a female artist (UK albums chart)' and 'Oldest artist to simultaneously top the UK singles and album charts'. Madonna was inducted to the Rock and Roll Hall of Fame and was named 'World's Wealthiest Female Musician' by *Forbes* magazine in 2008.

Madonna married actor Sean Penn in 1985. They divorced four years later. She then married director Guy Ritchie in 2000. They had a son. Madonna and Ritchie separated in 2008. Madonna is a mother of six children.

Madonna launched a short film, *secretprojectrevolution* at the Art of Freedom initiative in 2013. It aimed to promote free speech "to address persecution and injustice across the globe." She founded the Ray of Light Foundation in 1998.

She also co-founded a charitable organization, Raising Malawi. It works to provide health, education, and community support to vulnerable children in Malawi. In July 2017, she established a children's hospital called the Mercy James Institute for Pediatric Surgery and Intensive Care at the Queen Central Hospital in Malawi.

MARIAH CAREY

BIRTH: March 27, 1970
Huntington, New York, USA

Mariah Carey is an American pop singer and actor. She holds the record for the second-highest number one debuts in Billboard Hot 100. She is known for her five-octave range.

Carey was born in Huntington, Long Island, New York on 27th March, 1970. Her father, Alfred Roy Carey, is a Venezuelan aeronautical engineer. Her mother, Patricia Carey, is an Irish-American opera singer and voice coach. She has two elder siblings. Her parents divorced when Carey was three years old. Mariah Carey used to imitate her mother's opera singing from the age of two. She started taking singing lessons when she was four and began performing at the age of six.

Carey graduated from Harborfields High School in 1987. She moved to Manhattan to pursue her music career. She also worked as a waiter and a coat check girl.

In 1988, Mariah Carey signed a deal with Tommy Mottola, head of Columbia Records. Two years later, she released her self-titled debut album. The sales of this album were recorded to be about fifteen million worldwide. It contained four chart toppers. "Vision of Love", "Love Takes Time", "Some Day" and "I Don't Wanna Cry".

Her next album, 'Emotions' was released in 1991. It contained the songs "Can't Let Go" and "Make It Happen". In the same year, she did her MTV *Unplugged* version. It got triple-platinum certification from the Recording Industry Association of America (RIAA).

Carey's 1995 song "Fantasy" from the album 'Daydream' topped the music charts. This album also had the song "One Sweet Day" in collaboration with R&B group Boyz II Men. Her 1997 album 'Butterfly' contained her twelfth number one hit "Honey".

In 1998, Carey collaborated with Whitney Houston on the song "When You Believe" for the animated movie *Prince of Egypt*. Her 1999 album 'Rainbow' was certified as a triple-platinum album. Its single, "Heartbreaker" topped the charts. She then played a role in the 2001 movie *Glitter*.

In 2002, Carey signed a deal with Universal Music Group's Island/Def Jam Records. She released her album 'Charmbracelet' in the same year, which was a commercial failure. However, her 2005 album 'Emancipation of Mimi', became the top-selling album of the year in the US. It included the singles "We Belong Together" and "It's Like That". In 2008, Carey was the second, after The Beatles, to have the most number one hit singles in the U.S.

In 2009, she played a part in the movie *Precious*. Carey's 2010 album, 'Merry Christmas II You', became the top holiday album in the US. It was also recognized as the second Christmas album to top R&B/Hip-Hop charts. In 2011, she collaborated with Justin Bieber and re-recorded her famous 1994 song "All I Want for Christmas is You". In 2013, Carey also became one of the judges for the Fox television show, *American Idol*.

She performed her Vegas Show '#1 to Infinity' at Caesar's Palace in 2015. In the same year, she acted in and directed the movie *A Christmas Melody*. She also gave voice to the character "Mayor McCaskill" in the animated movie *The Lego Batman Movie* in 2017.

Carey won a Grammy Award in the category 'Best New Artist' in 1991. She received the Legend Award for the 'Best-Selling Female Pop Artist of the Millennium' in 2000. Carey ranked number one in MTV and *Blender* magazine's '22 Greatest Voices in Music' in 2003. In 2012, she ranked second in VH1's '100 Greatest Women in Music'.

Mariah Carey married Tommy Mottola in June 1993. They got a divorce in 1998. She then got married to actor Nick Cannon, in 2008, after he appeared in her music video for "Bye Bye". They had fraternal twins in 2011. Carey and Nick Cannon separated in 2016. Carey got engaged to Australian businessman James Packer in January 2016. However, they split up in October of the same year.

Carey is actively involved in various non-profit organizations. She helps The Fresh Air Fund in raising funds to provide free summer vacations to children from low-income houses in New York. She also co-founded Camp Mariah, an initiative of this organization. Other organizations that she is involved with include the World Hunger Relief Movement, Make-A-Wish Foundation, and the New York Presbyterian Hospital.

MICHAEL JACKSON

BIRTH: August 29, 1958
Gary, Indiana, USA

DEATH: June 25, 2009 (aged 50)
Los Angeles, California, USA

Michael Joseph Jackson was an African-American singer, dancer and recording artist. He is popularly referred to as the "King of Pop". His album 'Thriller' is the biggest seller of all times.

Michael Joseph Jackson was born in Gary, Indiana on 29th August, 1958. His mother,

Katherine Jackson, was a homemaker. His father, Joseph Jackson, was a crane operator at a steel plant. Michael Jackson was the seventh amongst nine siblings. Joseph Jackson had had musical ambitions for himself. He kept his aspirations alive through his children. They created a family band called the Jackson 5, when Michael was five years old. He became the group's lead vocalist. They even did local gigs at bars and clubs.

The band signed its first major record with Motown Records in 1969. Their first album, 'Diana Ross Presents the Jackson 5' was released in the December of 1969. They scored four consecutive number one pop hits with "I Want You Back," "ABC," "The Love You Save," and "I'll Be There" in 1970. Next year, they had a cartoon show titled after them. In 1976, the group withdrew their label from Motown Records. They changed their name to the Jacksons, and started production with Epic Records.

Michael Jackson produced his first solo album with music producer Quincy Jones in

1979. In 1979, his solo album 'Off The Wall' was released. It eventually sold twenty million copies all around the world. It had four singles in the US Top 10 Hits. In 1984, Michael Jackson did a final tour with his family band for their album 'Victory'.

Michael Jackson's second album, 'Thriller', came out in 1982. It is the largest-selling album in recording history. It made Jackson the first recording artist to simultaneously hold both the singles and album charts for both rhythm & blues, and pop. The album sold more than 38 million copies globally. The singles "Beat It", "Billie Jean" and "Thriller" belong to this album.

In the March of 1983, Michael Jackson performed on a TV special, *Motown 25*. He debuted his famous dance move—the moonwalk, while performing "Billie Jean". Other albums by Michael Jackson include 'Bad', 'Dangerous' and 'Invincible'. In 1988, he released an autobiography titled *Moonwalk*. It was also included in the *New York Times* best-seller list. During the 1980s,

Jackson became the talk of the nation for his allegedly frequent plastic surgeries and the skin pigment disease, vitiligo, which he claimed to have.

Michael Jackson bought a 2,700 acre property in Los Olivos, California in 1988. He named it Neverland. It was a fantasy retreat for him. His eighth album, 'Dangerous' came out in 1991 and became the bestselling album of the year worldwide. In 1992, Michael Jackson founded an organization called Heal the World. In the October of 2001, his last full-length album, 'Invincible', was released.

Michael Jackson has been included in the Guinness World Records thirty-nine times. He has been awarded fourteen Grammy Awards, including the Grammy Lifetime Achievement Award in 2010. He has also been honored with 26 American Music Awards. He has been inducted to the Rock and Roll Hall of Fame, Songwriters Hall of Fame, Dance Hall of Fame and Hollywood Hall of Fame.

Jackson married Lisa Marie Presley, daughter of the late Elvis Presley, in 1994. They separated after two years of marriage. He married Deborah Rowe in 1996. They had two children together. They divorced in 1999 and Jackson got full custody of the children. He had another child, Prince Michael "Blanket" Jackson II, through surrogacy.

On June 25, 2009, Michael Jackson passed away due to a cardiac arrest. On 7th July, 2009, a televised memorial was held at the Staples Center in Los Angeles. 17,500 free tickets were issued for this event. It had a viewership of one billion people, online and on TV. On 3rd September, 2009, a private funeral was held for him at the Forest Lawn Memorial Park in Glendale, California. There were memorials erected in his honor. One of them was erected at his childhood home in Gary, Indiana. The Lunar Republic Society renamed a crater on the moon after him.

In October 2009, *This Is It*—a documentary about Jackson's tour preparation—was released.

MICK JAGGER

BIRTH: July 26 1943
Dartford, Kent, England

Sir Michael Philip Jagger is a musician, songwriter, actor and producer. He founded the British band The Rolling Stones. Queen Elizabeth II knighted him in 2003.

Mick Jagger was born as Michael Phillip Jagger on 26th July, 1943. His father, Joe Jagger, was a physical education instructor. His mother, Eva Jagger, was a hairdresser. Jagger graduated from Dartford Grammar School and then was accepted to study Business at the

London School of Economics in 1962.

Jagger first realized that he was a performer when he was around 14. He would sit with rock bands without telling his parents. He would randomly perform some numbers and see how the crowd reacted. Sometimes, he even performed at family gatherings. His dad was furious when he told him that he wanted to leave the London School of Economics to become a full-time musician.

Jagger, Keith Richards, and Brian Jones went on to form The Rolling Stones. Later, Ian Stewart joined as a pianist. Charles Watt joined as a drummer in 1963 and Bill Wyman replaced Taylor on the bass.

The Stones started by creating covers of songs by other people. In 1964, their cover of Bobby Womack's "It's All Over Now" made it to the British charts. They released their self-titled album in the same year. Its single, "That Girl Belongs to Yesterday" became an

American hit. Their 1965 songs "The Last Time" and "I Can't Get No Satisfaction" topped the UK charts. Their album, 'Beggars Banquet' was released in 1968. Their 1968 single "Jumpin' Jack Flash" topped the UK charts and was in the top three in the US.

In the June of 1969, Brian Jones left the band. Mick Taylor replaced him. Jones was found dead on July 3, 1969. His death was considered "death by misadventure" in the official records. The Rolling Stones performed a free concert dedicated to Jones on July 5 of the same year. The concert was held at Hyde Park, London.

The album, 'Let It Bleed', was released in 1969. Their 1971 album, 'Sticky Fingers' contained the hit singles, "Brown Sugar" and "Wild Horses". They tried a different genre of music in their 1978 album, 'Some Girls'. Their 1994 album 'Voodoo Lounge' won the Grammy for the Best Rock Album.

Jagger decided to try his hand at being a

solo artist. He released his first solo album in 1985 called 'She's the Boss'. In 1987, his second solo album called 'Primitive Cool' was released. His third solo album, 'Wandering Spirits' was quite a commercial hit. His album 'Goddess in the Doorway' contained the hit song "Visions of Paradise". He also produced movies like *The Man from Elysian Fields*. His 2007 comedy production *The Knight of Prosperity* aired on ABC. He also produced *The Woman* in 2008.

Jagger formed a supergroup, 'SuperHeavy' in 2011, with Joss Stones, A.R. Rahman, Damian Marley and Dave Stewart. Jagger has performed for US President Barack Obama at the White House. On 25th March, 2016, the Stones performed at Havana, Cuba in a free concert for 500,000 people. Their music had earlier been banned there under the Communist regime.

Mick Jagger was inducted to the Rock and Roll Hall of Fame in 1989. In 2004, Jagger along with his bandmates, was inducted to the UK Music Hall of Fame. Jagger received knighthood in 2003 for his service in music. In 2005, he received the Golden Globe Award for "Old Habits Die Hard" in the 'Best Original Song' category.

Jagger is a fan of cricket. He founded the 'Jagged Internetworks' to "produce and promote sports and entertainment events on the Internet." Jay-Z's single, "Swagga Like Us" compliments Mick Jagger's vocal range with the lyrics "My swagger is Mick Jagger". Jagger is also the subject of Maroon 5's "Moves like Jagger".

In 1971, Jagger married Bianca Perez Morena de Macias. They got a divorce in 1980. Jagger married Jerry Hall in 1990. However, this marriage too was annulled in 1999. Jagger is a father of nine children.

MILES DAVIS

BIRTH: May 26, 1926
Alton, Illinois, USA

DEATH: September 28, 1991 (aged 65)
Santa Monica, California, USA

Miles Davis was an American jazz trumpeter, music composer and bandleader. He played a significant role in the development of jazz music. During his career, he experimented with the genre of rock music along with jazz.

Miles Davis was born as Miles Dewy Davis III on 26th May, 1926 in Alton, Illinois. His father, Miles II, was a dental surgeon. His mother, Cleota Henry, was a music teacher. He had two younger siblings.

His father gifted him the trumpet when he was thirteen years old. Elwood Buchanan was his mentor. He taught him to play the trumpet without vibrato. He later joined Eddie Randle's orchestra, Blue Devils.

In 1944, Davis attended Juilliard School (Institute of Musical Arts, then) in New York. In the following year, Davis decided to drop out of Juilliard and pursue a full-time career in music. He began to play with Charlie Parker's band. From 1945 to 1948, David recorded with Parker.

Davis formed the Miles Davis nonet with eight other musicians in 1948. They released many singles but went unnoticed. It was only with the compilation of major songs in the album, 'Birth of the Cool' that they gained recognition. These songs were considered to be new innovation in jazz music.

Davis's 'Miles Davis Quartet' was released in 1954. In 1954, Davis performed "Round Midnight" at the Newport Jazz Festival. He also formed a permanent troupe, The Great Quintet. Major recordings by the quintet include, 'Live at the Plugged Nickel', 'E.S.P.' and 'Miles Smiles'.

In 1959, Davis' album 'Kind of Blue' was released. It is also one of the largest-selling jazz albums.

His albums 'Miles Ahead', 'Porgy and Bess' and 'Sketches of Spain' were collaborations with Gil Evans. Davis' album 'Bitches Brew' was released in 1969. It marked the onset of the jazz fusion movement. His important albums from 1970 include 'Live-Evil' and the soundtrack 'A Tribute to Jack Johnson'.

In his 1985 album, 'You're Under Arrest', Davis interpreted songs by Michael Jackson and Cyndi Lauper.

Davis released his album 'Tutu' with Warner Bros. in 1986, for which he won a Grammy Award. His album, 'Aura', was released in 1989. He won another Grammy Award for this.

Davis also acted in movies like *Scrooged* and *Dingo*. Davis published his autobiography *Miles: The Autobiography* with Quincy Troupe in 1989. In 1991, Davis played with Quincy Jones at the Montreux Jazz Festival.

Miles Davis has been awarded eight Grammy Awards. He even received the Lifetime Achievement Award in 1990. He was honored with a star on the Hollywood Walk of Fame in 1998. Davis was inducted to the Rock and Roll Hall of Fame and honored as "one of the key figures in the history of jazz". He was bestowed with France's highest civilian honor, the Chevalier de la Legion d'Honneur, in Paris. He was also inducted to the St Louis Walk of Fame in 1990.

Davis married several times, but all of them ended in divorce. His last marriage was to the American actor, Cicely Tyson, in 1981. They got divorced in 1989. He fathered four children.

Davis passed away on 28th September, 1991, due to respiratory failure and pneumonia. He was 65 years old.

He was also called the "Prince of Darkness" due to his personality and voice. He participated in anti-apartheid albums to show his support against racist policies. His last album,'Doo-Bop' was released posthumously in 1992. Davis also received his last Grammy Award for his recording with Quincy Jones in 1993, posthumously. He is considered to be one of the most influential jazz musicians in history, with the likes of Louis Armstrong, Duke Ellington and Charlie Parker.

PRINCE

BIRTH: June 7, 1958
Minneapolis, Minnesota, USA

DEATH: April 21, 2016 (aged 57)
Chanhassen, Minnesota, USA

Prince was an American singer, songwriter, record producer and filmmaker. He has sold millions of albums all around the world. He was one of the bestselling music artists of all times.

Prince was born Prince Rogers Nelson on 7th June, 1958. His father, John Nelson, was a musician with the stage name of Prince Rogers. His mother, Mattie Shaw, was a jazz singer. Prince started playing the piano at the age of seven.

He even learned to play the guitar and drums by himself.

In 1978, Prince signed a record deal with Warner Bros. Records. His debut album 'For You' was released in 1978. The following year, his self- titled album was released. The hit singles from this album are "I Wanna Be Your Lover" and "Why You Wanna Treat Me So Bad?" His 1981 album was 'Controversy'. Prince gained international recognition with his 1982 album titled '1999'. Its songs "Little Red Corvette" and "Delirious" became Top 10 hits.

He released his 1984 album, 'Purple Rain' with his band Revolution. It was also the soundtrack for a movie with the same name. It won the Academy Award in the category of 'Best Original Song Score'. The title track of this album was number two on the Billboard Hot 100. Moreover, its songs, "When Doves Cry" and "Let's Go Crazy", reached number one. Prince's 'Around the World in a Day' was released in 1985. It contained the songs "Raspberry Beret" and "Pop Life", which featured in Top 10 lists. His 1986 single "Kiss" became the number one pop/R&B song.

The album 'Parade' was the soundtrack to his film *Under the Cherry Moon,* in which he acted and directed. The title track of his 1987 album 'Sign 'O' the Times' reached number three on pop charts and number one on R&B charts. In 1989, Prince gave the soundtrack for the movie *Batman*. The song "Partyman" was in the Top 5 R&B hits, while "Batdance" was number one on the Top 100 charts.

Prince launched his backing band, the New Power Generation, in the 1990s. They gave the soundtrack to the movie *Graffiti Bridge*. The song "Thieves in the Temple" was placed in the Top 10 tracks. The 1991 album, 'Diamonds and Pearls' ranked number three on the Billboard 200 chart and was a major success.

Prince signed a $100 million record deal with Warner Bros. in 1992. It was considered "the largest recording and music publishing contract in history" at the time. Prince released 'Love Symbol Album' in 1992 with the New Power Generation. He changed his name to a symbol that was a mixture of the male and female symbols. This symbol was also referred to as the love symbol. He used this name until the year 2000.

Prince's 1995 album 'The Gold Experience' contained the Top-5 song "The Most Beautiful Girl in the World". In 1996, his album 'Emancipation' was certified platinum. Other albums by Prince include, 'Crystal Ball', 'Rave Un2 the Joy Fantastic'.

Prince performed with Beyoncé Knowles at the Grammy Awards, in 2004, after years of relative absence from the spotlight. He was inducted to the Rock and Roll Hall of Fame in the same year. In 2004, his album 'Musicology' was also released. It won a Grammy Award. In 2006, he released the album '3121'. He also wrote and sang "Song of the Heart" for the animated movie *Happy Feet* that year. It won him a Golden Globe in the category of 'Best Original Song'.

Prince was awarded the Academy Award for 'Purple Rain' in the category of 'Best Original Score' in 1985. He has won eight Grammy Awards including 'Best Traditional R&B performance' for 'Musicology'. His album 'Sign 'O' the Times' was inducted to the Grammy Hall of Fame in 2017.

Prince married Mayte Garcia in 1996. Their child was born with genetic complications and lived for a week. They got a divorce in 2000. Prince married Manuela Testolini in 2001. They too separated in 2006.

On April 21, 2016, Prince was found dead in his home at Paisley Park. He was 57 years old. In October, Prince's home at Paisley Park was officially converted into a museum. His first posthumous song was "Moonbeam Levels". The development of a documentary based on his life began soon after. It is titled *Prince: R U Listening?*

STEVIE WONDER

BIRTH: May 13, 1950
Saginaw, Michigan, USA

Stevie Wonder is an American singer, song-writer and multi-instrumentalist. He was a child prodigy, making his recording debut at age eleven.

Stevie Wonder was born Steveland Judkins on 13th May, 1950 at Saginaw, Michigan. Wonder was born six weeks premature and and exposure to pure oxygen in the incubator might have caused his loss of vision. His father, Calvin Judkins, and mother, Lula Mae, got a divorce when he was four years old.

At the age of eleven, he was discovered by Ronnie White of The Miracles. He then auditioned before the founder of Motown Records, Berry Gordy, Jr. He got a record deal with them immediately. He was renamed Little Stevie Wonder by Berry Gordy, Jr. Wonder worked with Clarence Paul to produce his debut album 'The Jazz Soul of Little Stevie Wonder' in 1962, an instrumental album. In the same year, he released 'Tribute to Uncle Ray', which included covers of songs by Ray Charles.

Wonder's album 'Recorded Live: The 12 Year Old Genius' contained the single, "Fingertips". The edited "Fingertips, Pt. 2" reached the number one spot on the R&B and pop charts. Wonder dropped "Little" from his name around the 1960s. His single "Uptight (Everything's Alright)" became number one on the R&B charts. His cover of Bob Dylan's "Blowin' in the Wind" also topped the R&B charts. His album 'My Cherie Amour' was released in 1969. Its single "Yester-Me, Yester-You, Yesterday" was ranked in the Top 5 R&B.

In 1971, Wonder released his album, 'Where I'm Coming From'. Its Single, "If You Really Love Me" was a huge hit. In the March of 1972, he released the album 'Music of My Mind'.

His 1972 album, 'Talking Book' contained two hit singles, "Superstition" and "You Are the Sunshine of My Life". From his 1973 album, 'Innervisions', the singles "Higher Ground" and "Living for the City" topped the R&B charts. His 1974 single, "You Haven't Done Nothin'" topped both the pop and R&B charts and featured The Jackson 5.

In 1980, his album 'Hotter Than July' was released. Its song "Master Blaster (Jammin')" was a tribute to Bob Marley. In 1984, Wonder gave the soundtrack for the movie *The Woman in Red*, by Gene Wilder. Number one R&B hits from 'Character' include "Skeletons" and "You Will Know".

In 1991, Wonder gave the soundtrack to Spike Lee's movie, *Jungle Fever*. His 1995 album, 'Conversation Peace', contained the smashing hits, "Tomorrow Robins Will Sing" and "For You Love", for which he won two Grammy awards.

Stevie Wonder has been awarded 25 Grammy Awards in his lifetime. Wonder was inducted to the Songwriters Hall of Fame in 1983. He won the Academy Award for "I Just Called to Say I Love You" in 1985. He was honored in the Rock and Roll Hall of Fame in 1989. Wonder received the Lifetime Achievement Award in 1996.

He received the Polar Music Prize and Kennedy Center Honor in 1999. The Songwriters Hall of Fame granted him the Sammy Cahn Lifetime Achievement Award in 2002. He was awarded the Billboard Century Award in 2004. In 2006, Wonder was inducted to the Michigan Walk of Fame. He was honored as a United Nations Messenger of Peace in 2009. Wonder also received the Presidential Medal of Freedom in 2014.

Stevie Wonder married Syreeta Wright in 1970. They got divorced two years later. They also had a son in 1977, named Keita.

Wonder then married fashion designer, Kai Millard Morris, in 2001. They separated in 2012. He married Tomeeka Robyn Bracy in 2017. He has 9 children.

WHITNEY HOUSTON

BIRTH: *August 9, 1963*
Newark, New Jersey, USA

DEATH: *February 11, 2012 (aged 48)*
Beverly Hills, California, USA

Whitney Houston was an American singer and actress. She is one of the best-selling musicians of the 1980s and 90s.

Whitney Houston was born on 9th August, 1963 at Newark, New Jersey. She is the daughter of Emily "Cissy" Houston and John R. Houston. Her mother was an American soul and gospel singer. Her mother's group, Sweet Inspirations, sang backup for the legendary Aretha Franklin.

Whitney sang in the choir at New Hope Baptist Church, which was managed by her mother. Houston was a backup singer for the Michael Zager band in 1977. She also sang backup for Chaka Khan's "I'm Every Woman" in 1978. Houston started getting record deals and modeling contracts at the age of fifteen. She was one of the first African-American women to be featured in *Seventeen* magazine.

Houston was discovered by Clive Davis, president of Arista Records at the age of nineteen. He signed her on immediately. Davis and Houston spent the following years in search of producers and lyricists for her. Houston had her debut on national television on The Merv Griffin Show and sang "Home" from the musical *The Wiz*.

Whitney's debut album 'Whitney Houston' was released in 1985 and was a major pop sensation. It contained three hit singles: "Greatest Love of All", "Saving All My Love for

You", and "How Will I Know". Houston won a Grammy for "Saving All My Love for You" in 1985. Her second album 'Whitney', was released in 1987. It was certified platinum. Houston won a Grammy for the single "I Wanna Dance With Somebody (Who Loves Me)" from this album. Houston performed at the concert for Nelson Mandela's birthday while on a world tour for 'Whitney'.

Whitney Houston made her debut in the movies with *The Bodyguard* in 1992. Houston recorded her version of Dolly Parton's 1974 "I Will Always Love You" for this movie, which turned out to be the biggest hit of her career. She received a Grammy Award for this in the category 'Record of the Year'. She also starred in other movies including, *Waiting to Exhale* and *The Preacher's Wife*. The soundtrack of *The Preacher's Wife* became one of the best-selling gospel albums of all time.

Houston's 'My Love Is Your Love' album was

released in 1998. Its single "It's Not Right but It's Okay" won her another Grammy Award. She collaborated with Mariah Carey for the single "When You Believe", for the movie The Prince of Egypt. She won an Academy Award for this song.

Whitney released her album 'I Look to You' in 2009 which debuted at the number one spot on Billboard 200. Its single "Million Dollar Bill" was quite a hit.

Houston has won six Grammy Awards throughout her career. She has been awarded the Billboard Music Awards sixteen times, and the American Music Awards twenty-one times. She was recognized as the most awarded female musician of all time, by Guinness World Records, in 2009. Houston is the only singer to have had seven consecutive number ones at the Billboard Hot 100. She ranked third in MTV's list of '22 Greatest Voices'. In 2013, Houston was inducted to the New Jersey Hall of Fame. In the following year, she got inducted to the Rhythm and Blues Music Hall of Fame.

Houston created the Whitney Houston Foundation for Children to support children's organizations such as Caudwell Children and the Children's Defense Fund. She also supported the American Foundation for AIDS Research and the Celebrity Fight Night Foundation. The Hearing and Language Disorder Clinic of the National Birth Defects Center has been renamed to the Whitney Houston Hearing and Language Disorder Clinic in Boston.

Houston married Bobby Brown in 1992. They had a daughter together named Bobbi Kristina. They divorced in 2007. Houston gained full custody of her daughter. Whitney Houston passed away on 11th February, 2012, in a bathtub at the Beverly Hilton hotel. She was 48 years old. Official records state the cause of her death to be accidental drowning.

A documentary, about her life, *Whitney*, was released in 2018. It premiered at the Cannes Film Festival. *Whitney: Can I Be Me* is a documentary directed by Nick Broomfield which was screened in 2017.

WOLFGANG AMADEUS MOZART

BIRTH: *January 27, 1756*
Salzburg, Austria

DEATH: *December 5, 1791*
Vienna, Austria

Wolfgang Amadeus Mozart was a popular and prolific music composer of the classical period. He has created over 600 compositions that include sonatas, symphonies, operas, chamber music and concertos.

Johann Chrysostom Wolfgang Amadeus Mozart, baptized as Johannes Chrysostomus Wolfgangus Theophilus Mozart, was born on 27th January, 1756, to Leopold Mozart and Anna Maria Pertl. Leopold was musically inclined. He was a composer and an author who wrote about violin playing, and was a part of the court of the archbishop of Salzburg.

Leopold Mozart taught music and academics to his children. Mozart played the piano, the violin and other instruments.

Wolfgang gave his first musical performance at the age of six, in the Bavarian court in Munich. Wolfgang and his sister, Nannerl, went on to perform in the courts of London, Paris, Zurich and The Hague.

At the age of seventeen, Wolfgang Mozart was made an assistant concert-master at Salzburg, by Prince Archbishop Hieronymus von Colloredo. Mozart wrote five violin concertos during this time. He then shifted his focus to piano concertos.

In 1777, Wolfgang Mozart resigned from his position at the court of Salzburg. He went on trips to Munich, Augsburg, and Mannheim. Mozart did find several employment opportunities but nothing promising. He was in debt and had to pawn goods in order to meet his expenses. In 1778, Mozart's mother died. The next year, Wolfgang went back to Salzburg, where his father had got him a position at the court as an organist.

Wolfgang Mozart wrote an opera for Munich, *Idomeneo* in 1781. In March of the same year, Mozart was summoned to Vienna by Archbishop von Colloredo. Mozart was treated like a servant and was extremely underpaid. He felt disrespected and resigned from his post. He began composing the opera '*Die Entfuhrung aus dem Serail*' (*The Abduction from the Seraglio*). This opera premiered on 16th July, 1782. He also gave performances as a pianist.

Johannes Sebastian Bach and George Frederic Handel inspired Mozart to work with the Baroque style of composition. He composed a mass in C minor. "Kyrie" and "Gloria" were its first two and only completed sections. In 1783, Mozart went to visit his home at Salzburg with his family.

Mozart composed six quartets dedicated to Joseph Haydn from 1782 to 1785. In 1786, he collaborated with the librettist Lorenzo Da Ponte to produce the operas, *The Marriage of Figaro* and *Don Giovanni*. These are considered to be two of his most important works. Both the operas are appreciated for bringing a connection between music and drama. Mozart had also started keeping a catalogue of his compositions.

Emperor Joseph II appointed Mozart as his chamber composer in the December of 1787. Mozart then composed his last three symphonies (39, 40 and 41) and the last of the three Da Ponte operas. He would borrow money from his friends, mainly Mason Michael Puchberg, to meet the expenses.

1790-91 are considered to be his most productive years. He composed the opera *The Magical Flute* at this time. He also created a piano concerto in B-flat, clarinet concerto in A major and an unfinished Requiem K.626.

His health began to deteriorate in the September of 1791. On 5th December, 1791, he passed away, at the age of 35. The cause of his death was rheumatic inflammatory fever.

Mozart married Constanze Weber on 4th August, 1782. They had six children, but only two children, Karl Thomas and Franz Xaver, survived.

QUESTIONS

Q.1. What's the English translation for A.R. Rahman's "Satayameva Jayate"?

Q.2. Name the record label that Whitney Houston signed a deal in 1983.

Q.3. What was Bob Marley's full name?

Q.4. In which year did David Bowie release his first album?

Q.5. What was the first record company Aretha Franklin recorded for?

Q.6. Elton John began working as a staff songwriter at which British record label in 1968?

Q.7. Which Biblical characters are mentioned in Bob Dylan's song "Desolation Row"?

Q.8. Which sports team did Elton John purchase in 1977?

Q.9. Where was A.R. Rahman born? Briefly describe his childhood.

Q.10. Which is Madonna's best-selling album to date?

Q.11. What honor did Bob Marley receive in March of 1994?

Q.12. In which band was Whitney Houston the lead singer, in 1977?

Q.13. Which year did Aretha Franklin sign with Atlantic records?

Q.14. What was Bob Dylan's first album called?

Q.15. Which song by James Brown was a hit single in 1972?

Q.16. What was Beethoven's first name?

Q.17. When was John Lennon born?

Q.18. Who was Elton John? Give a brief description.

Q.19. What was the first formal band that Jimi Hendrix played with?

Q.20. Who is popularly referred to as the 'King of Pop'?

Q.21. Which hit single did Little Stevie Wonder have in 1963?

Q.22. With whom did Elvis Presley sign his record deal in 1955? What was the name of his first hit?

Q.23. Who wrote songs for the Disney movie The Lion King with Tim Rice in 1990?

Q.24. Who wrote the album 'Emotions', which released in 1992?

Q.25. Who was John Lennon?

Q.26. What the name of Mick Jagger's band?

Q.27. Who were the members of Band of Gypsys?

Q.28. What was the name of Stevie Wonder's first album, released in 1963?

Q.29. Who were some of Beethoven's classical peers?

Did You Know?

1. 'Music Box', Mariah Carey's third album from 1993, has "Hero" on its track list, the song for which Carey is best known.

2. Aretha Franklin's career is well over 50 years in the making, so she has seen quite a few American presidents in her time. She was even invited to sing at three different inauguration ceremonies.

3. Whitney Houston still holds the title of the best-selling single by a woman. "I Will Always Love You" re-entered the Billboard charts after her death.

4. Bowie's "Space Oddity," was released on July 11, 1969, just five days before the Apollo 11 moon launch.

5. Madonna is also the author of ten children's books. Her most popular one is *Friends for Life*!

6. John Lennon was posthumously inducted into the Songwriters Hall of Fame and to the Rock and Roll Hall of Fame.

7. In 1990, Madonna was nominated to get a

star on the Hollywood Walk of Fame, but she turned it down.

8. In high school, Prince played football, basketball and baseball despite being short.

9. In 2001, Michael Jackson spoke at the Oxford Union about child welfare as part of his 'Heal the Kids' initiative.

10. Aretha Franklin had an asteroid named after her in 2014 called 249516 Aretha.

11. Mariah Carey was named the 'Best Selling Female Artist of the Millennium' at the World Music Awards.

12. When London hosted the Olympics in 2012, Bowie turned down the opportunity to perform live his ballad "Heroes" for the closing ceremony.

13. Mercury was well known for performing with a "bottomless mic" during his live shows.

14. In 1979, Mercury proved his status as a Renaissance man by joining the Royal Ballet for a charity gala performance.